Workbook

For

Brené Brown's

Atlas of the Heart

Mapping Meaningful Connection and the Language of Human Experience

Smart Reads

Note to readers:
This is an unofficial workbook for Brené Brown's "Atlas of the Heart: Mapping Meaningful Connection and the Language of Human Experience" designed to enrich your reading experience. The original book can be purchased on Amazon.

Download Your Free Gift

As a way to say "Thank You" for being a fan of our series, I've included a free gift for you:

Brain Health: How to Nurture and Nourish Your Brain For Top Performance

Go to www.smart-reads.com to get your FREE book.

The Smart Reads Team

Table of Contents

Overview of *Atlas of the Heart*

For centuries now, researchers and behavioral scientists have been delving deep into the human psyche, trying to understand how we think, analyze, and learn. But what about how we *feel*? *Atlas of the Heart* is bestselling author Brené Brown's newest, most groundbreaking endeavor, in which she explores 87 different feelings – what she declares to be every human emotion and experience.

Atlas of the Heart compiles similar emotions by chapter, in order to organize and give direction to the reader. You will learn about the "places we go," as the author puts it, whether we are feeling lost, disconnected, and angry or joyful, grateful, and basking in life's wonders – and every emotion in between!

There are overarching themes of language, intention, and relationships, as they relate back to emotion and human experience. The author makes it a point to describe the difference between very similar emotions, such as jealousy and envy or awe and wonder. By examining the differences as well as the similarities, and by identifying each emotion as a "state" or a "trait", this book is an excellent way to intensely scrutinize the pathways of your own emotional journey without hiding, avoiding, or refusing to acknowledge the uncomfortable truths that may be revealed.

Understanding why we feel the things we do, and the context surrounding these emotions, is hugely important for us as we journey through our lives. Thoroughly absorbing this book – which may take multiple read-throughs – will help you become a more nuanced, tolerant, and stronger person. Approach this incredibly impactful book with an open heart and mind, allowing it to settle deep within and change the way you view your emotions and those of others around you.

This book is not for the faint of heart. It will jolt your awareness of your own feelings and cause you to question the acceptance of long-held beliefs about emotions. Most of all, it will allow you to identify the root causes of unhealthy feelings to help you on your journey toward healing and wholeness.

Introduction

In the introduction to her book, Brené Brown gives us some important context for the chapters to come. Brown is a research professor and expert on human emotions. As a child, Brown did not live in a physically abusive home, but she did experience emotional distance from her parents. As a result, she learned some unhealthy coping mechanisms and communication skills, which would plague her until she began her research for this book. By the time her research was concluded, she had cataloged and explored 87 different human emotions and experiences.

Some of the broader conclusions she came to included how each of us acts and how that relates back to how we think and feel. Brown shares that, in her earlier years, she suffered from an addiction to alcohol. She explored how unhealthy (and even, sometimes, healthy) coping mechanisms can cloud our observational skills and decision-making abilities and affect our quality of life. She was able to come to the difficult conclusion that her addiction was not serving her well. In fact, it was harming her ability to think and see clearly.

This is true of any sort of "numbing" coping mechanism — alcohol, drug use, adrenaline-seeking behaviors, gambling, overindulging, and the list goes on. Brown, after becoming sober, realized the more someone uses a numbing agent to cope with stress, the less of a connection she has with herself and her heart.

Emotional temperament is a huge part of how we are defined and see ourselves as people. The more emotionally literate we become, the better we are able to communicate with others and get the things we want out of life. One major hallmark of an emotionally stunted person is that they will inflict pain on others, even their own loved ones, if it means they themselves can avoid emotional pain. This is all too prevalent in our society, and it is totally avoidable. It must be addressed in order to improve our relationships with those around us.

Lessons from the Introduction:

- Substance abuse is a warning sign, indicating that the addicted person has ongoing trouble with feeling and expressing their emotions, so they use numbing agents to cope and calm themselves.

- The research is still underway for many of the emotions discussed in this guide.

- Understanding how and why we feel a certain way is instrumental to becoming a healthier, happier person.

Chapter One: Places We Go When Things Are Uncertain or Too Much

Summary

Chapter one discusses the following emotions and experiences: stress, overwhelm, anxiety, worry, avoidance, excitement, dread, fear, and vulnerability.

As with all of the emotions discussed in this book, they can either be a state (situation) or a trait (part of our personality). Some of them exist as both a state and a trait.

Stress and overwhelm are certainly similar emotions, but there is one fundamental difference. When we are stressed, we are dealing with a difficult – but manageable – situation, which *can be overcome* with effort. Constant stress is unhealthy and, if we are constantly succumbing to stress, we are putting a lot of strain on our bodies. However, being overwhelmed means something entirely different.

Being overwhelmed means we are in a situation that is unmanageable, no matter how much effort we put forth.

This is when we surrender and ask for help. Overwhelm happens when situations and problems arise more quickly than we are able to handle or even process them.

Anxiety is both a state and a trait, in which something is scary, unpredictable, and does not make sense to us logically, but still leaves us terrorized. We feel unable to get through the situation without experiencing relief.

Anxiety is an emotion and a state that all of us have experienced during our lives. Anxiety will lead to worrying – but, as it turns out, worrying is not actually an emotion. Worry is a response to a real or perceived threat.

An anxiety disorder is different from the usual, normal feelings of occasional anxiety. Disordered anxiety is also a trait, rather than a state.

Having an anxiety disorder means the feelings of anxiety are long-term and accompanied by a host of other symptoms, like trouble concentrating, fatigue, sleeplessness, and a loss of appetite, for example.

Interestingly, excitement can actually feel just like anxiety, depending on the lens it is viewed through. If the unpredictable event is actually something good, rather than scary, you will interpret the experience as excitement, which can often coexist with anxiety.

Fear is a short-term emotion, felt briefly and strongly.

Fear is also different from anxiety. We experience fear when the threat is real and imminent. It causes our nervous system to present us with three options: fight, flight, or freeze. Most of us use avoidance to prevent fear, dread, and anxiety. This is a short-term solution that will not actually solve the problem.

Finally, vulnerability is what we feel during times of uncertainty. We are not sure how something will go, and we feel exposed, worried, and anxious until the uncertainty vanishes. Examples of feeling vulnerable include opening ourselves up emotionally to another person, conceiving after a miscarriage, or facing daunting work situations.

Vulnerability is not a weakness.

In fact, by facing our own insecurities and most vulnerable feelings, we are demonstrating invaluable courage.

Key Points

1. Stress, overwhelm, and anxiety often go hand in hand – these are all negative emotions, which are largely misunderstood or mistaken for weaknesses.

2. Anxiety is extremely complicated. It can manifest as a trait, a state, or a disorder. Oftentimes, anxiety can even feel like excitement, causing emotional confusion.

3. Fear, dread, and vulnerability also go hand in hand, but they occur in response to outside stimuli.

4. Vulnerability should not be equated with weakness.

Questions to Guide the Reader

1. What are the three main responses to feeling fear?

_____
_____
_____
_____

2.   How are excitement and anxiety alike and how are they different?

_____

_____

_____

_____

3. Should vulnerability be pursued? Why?

_____

_____

_____

_____

Action Plan

1. Learn how to distinguish between the negative emotions of stress and overwhelm. Being overly stressed is neither pleasant nor healthy, but you know you will ultimately arrive at a solution. Overwhelm, on the other hand, is a state of complete shutdown.

2. If you suffer from anxiety, it is worth exploring with a therapist or psychologist. Some anxiety is normal in day-to-day life, but if anxiety has taken over parts of your life, or your entire life, there is help available!

3. There are a lot of people who wish to lead – at their jobs, in their communities, etc. Remember that accepting vulnerability is a key component of being a strong leader.

Chapter Two: Places We Go When We Compare

Summary

The emotions discussed in this chapter are comparison, admiration, reverence, envy, jealousy, resentment, schadenfreude, and freudenfreude.

The first – comparison – is not actually an emotion at all. We do not feel it; it actually happens *to* us.

However, comparison does lead to a lot of other complex emotions, like jealousy, resentment, and envy. It will also lead to conflicting feelings of both wanting to fit in and to stand out. Regardless of whom or what we are comparing ourselves to, allowing your mind to accept these comparisons will only lead to anger, fear, sadness, and shame.

Admiration, by contrast, is a lovely emotion that comes from feeling inspired, or by seeing or experiencing beauty.

Reverence, while similar to admiration, has an element of worship to it. We can admire something that we do not revere as divine.

Envy and jealousy, despite often being used simultaneously, are different emotions.

Jealousy is the fear of losing something we already have (example: a romantic partner, or a coveted job title), and envy is the desire of wanting something we do not already have that someone else does (example: aspiring to the coveted job that is already occupied, lusting after someone who is married).

Envy can have undertones of hostility, but is generally a harmless emotion that all of us experience at some point. Jealousy is also a normal emotion, but can, of course, be harmful if allowed to fester.

Resentment is a subset of *envy*, not anger, as some people may incorrectly believe.

When we feel resentment, it means we are upset with ourselves for having failed to do something, e.g., failed to set a boundary or failed to set realistic expectations. You may resent that fourth person in your group project for seemingly "not working hard enough," but what we often fail to see is that the reason we feel this is because we are envious of that person for feeling secure in their work, when we ourselves do not, due to unrealistic expectations.

Schadenfreude and freudenfreude are German words used to describe similar emotions.

Schadenfreude refers to the peculiar emotion of deriving pleasure from someone else's misfortune or defeat.

This is the exact opposite of empathy – is actually counter-empathy – and should be checked and examined. It is part of the human experience and we will all feel this way at some point, but it is important not to let these types of emotions have free reign.

Freudenfreude is the exact opposite - the emotion of deriving pleasure from someone else's success.

This is empathy. In fact, some people feel as though serious mental health disorders, such as Major Depressive Disorder, can actually erode our ability to feel this type of empathy for others. This is an emotion that should be celebrated and nurtured.

Key Points

1. When we compare ourselves to others, there are often many more negative consequences than positive ones.

2. Judgment, resentment, anger, shame, and bitterness all come from feelings of insecurity in ourselves.

3. Envy and jealousy are *different* emotions. One relates to wanting to keep something we have, while the other is the feeling of coveting something belonging to someone else.

4. Schadenfreude and freudenfreude are German words that mean the opposite emotions of empathy and counter-empathy.

Questions to Guide the Reader

1. How are jealousy and envy different? How are they the same? What sort of language is used concerning these emotions, and how should it be changed?

_____

_____

_____

_____

2. What is resentment, and how does it relate to
    anger and envy? Which is it more closely related
    to?

_____

_____

_____

_____

3. What is counter-empathy?

_____

_____

_____

_____

Action Plan

1. Whenever you feel jealous of someone, you should
    question yourself to determine whether you are
    jealous or envious. The difference will change what
    type of resolution the conflict will have. Jealousy
    occurs when someone close to you is taking time,
    resources, or attention away and giving it to
    someone or something else. Envy occurs when we
    covet something that someone else has, which we

want to have for ourselves. It's a nuanced difference, but an important one.

2. During times of resentment, try to overcome this negative, consuming emotion by asking yourself "What is it this person has or is doing that I covet?" The answer will depend on whether you want to admit it or not.

3. Empathy and counter-empathy are powerful. While it may be easy to temporarily revel in someone's misfortune, this is ultimately a harmful emotion. Practice empathy instead: think of a sports team. The person who scored the goal should always be grateful for those who helped them score. And when empathy is practiced regularly, those same people will celebrate your assistance as well. Empathy creates lasting connections, and counter-empathy destroys them.

Chapter Three: Places We Go When Things Don't Go as Planned

Summary

This chapter discusses boredom, disappointment, expectations, regret, discouragement, resignation, and frustration.

Boredom, to start out with, is an uncomfortable emotion, born from a lack of stimulation.

Boredom is not necessarily a bad thing – it can prompt creativity and imagination.

Some people think boredom is the reason for creative ventures – as a cure. However, boredom can also lead to lethargy, depression, and frustration, depending on how much control we have over our lack of stimulation.

If the situation is one in which we have control over our circumstances, but choose not to stimulate ourselves, we may become depressed and lethargic. However, if the circumstances surrounding our boredom are out of our control, we are likely to become frustrated or even frantic.

Disappointment is the emotion we feel when we have not met someone else's expectations or – even worse – when we have not met our own expectations. We can also be disappointed in another person for not meeting our expectations.

The higher the stakes of the expectations, the deeper and more profound the disappointment.

Disappointment is complicated. It can be avoided, but that often involves lowering expectations. If we do so and the expectations originally set were realistic and achievable, then we are not curing disappointment, we are avoiding it. Not to mention that, when we lower expectations to a point where one cannot be disappointed, we will not be able to fully engage and enjoy life to its fullest.

Sometimes we are dealing with "stealth emotions." The author describes this as a phenomenon when we believe that we and others have the same picture of expectations in our heads. When someone else fails to meet those expectations, we feel disappointed, even though we did not discuss them with the other person beforehand.

Sometimes, there is an element of low self-esteem. How can we ask someone for something we need if we don't feel we deserve it?

Regret is similar to disappointment, but comes when we feel our expectations were not met because of something we did or failed to do, or a decision we made. Regret should be thought of as a teaching emotion – it is a reminder for us to change, reflect, and grow.

Discouragement is different from resignation, much in the same way that anxiety and overwhelm are different.

Discouragement occurs when we feel weary and lose confidence. Resignation is the emotion that comes from a loss of confidence, along with the *inability* to go on. Not just feeling weary, but losing the desire to continue.

Finally, as touched on above, frustration is the emotion we feel when our circumstances are out of our control, and we cannot effectively make a change or proceed with a situation.

Key Points

1. Disappointment is a complex emotion. As the scale of unmet expectations rises, so do the negative feelings of disappointment.

2. Regret is a form of empathy – it guides us to change our behavior and grow.

3. Negative feelings arising from unmet expectations can range from disappointment, regret, and discouragement to resignation and frustration.

Questions to Guide the Reader

1. What emotion do we feel when we have a certain idea of how something will happen, and it does not happen that way?

_____

_____

_____

_____

2. Is there a way to avoid disappointment? (Careful, trick question!)

_____

_____

_____

_____

3. How are resentment and regret different?

_____

_____

_____

_____

Action Plan

1. Practice avoiding disappointment by being honest about your expectations. Always check in with others to find out their expectations to be sure they align with yours.

2. If someone shares excitement, hopes, dreams, or aspirations with you, be sure to thank them for being honest and open. It takes a lot of courage to share these things and, should they lead to disappointment, they will need support from those closest to them.

3. Know the difference between discouragement and resignation – discouragement is salvageable. Once someone is completely resigned, however, a major change in their expectations and, likewise, your expectations of them, must occur.

Chapter Four: Places We Go When It's Beyond Us

Summary

This chapter examines awe, wonder, confusion, curiosity, interest, and surprise.

We must again point out the difference between two of these related emotions: awe and wonder. They are often used as synonyms, but are actually two different emotions.

Wonder usually has an element of inspiring us to copy, create, or understand. For example, a young painter studying an older, more successful painting may feel wonder, leading him to understand and copy the techniques in the older painting.

Awe is the simple appreciation for something strange, wonderful, or enormous.

Think of staring up at the sky. You may also feel wonder, but mostly you will feel awe in the hugeness of the sky. Both of these emotions fuel our imagination and should be considered very positive and instructive emotions.

Confusion is a learning experience. Feeling slight confusion will fuel us to further study or try to understand something. However, feeling too much confusion can lead to stress and frustration.

Curiosity and interest are similar, but they are not the same. Interest is a cognitive emotion, and it exists as a state, not a trait. Someone cannot have a personality trait known as "interested in things." In fact, that personality trait would likely be closer to someone who is curious by nature. Curiosity can be a trait or a state. We can feel curious about something, and we can also hold curiosity in our hearts as a facet of who we are.

Curiosity can lead to interest, and interest can lead to curiosity, but it must be understood that these are actually different emotions.

Surprise is a reaction to something unexpected happening. True surprise only lasts a few seconds.

Key Points

1. Awe and wonder belong to the same family of emotions, but they are different. Wonder inspires us to understand, while awe is an appreciation for something amazing and wondrous.

2. Curiosity and interest are also similar, but they differ in where the emotion comes from and to where it leads – curiosity often leads to interest, and interest can lead to curiosity, in an endless loop.

3. Surprise is a seconds-long, intense burst of emotion, which often leads us to investigate and reconcile what we thought was true combined with the unexpected element of surprise.

Questions to Guide the Reader

1. What is the difference between curiosity and interest? How can one lead to the other?

    _____
    _____
    _____
    _____

2. Does curiosity fade as we grow older?

    _____
    _____
    _____
    _____

3. What does surprise do to us?

    _____
    _____
    _____
    _____

Action Plan

1. Pay attention to curiosity and wonder, as they will fuel your imagination and stimulate your continued interest in learning.

2. The state of awe is generally pleasant, but if it dredges up feelings of vulnerability, it's important to steer yourself toward interest in the topic, rather than embarrassment about a gap in knowledge.

3. When one is truly surprised, it can lead to anxiety and frustration, or it can lead to interest and curiosity. Be careful how you interpret surprise! Sometimes a surprise will result in negative emotions, which we must learn to manage.

Chapter Five: Places We Go When Things Aren't What They Seem

Summary

This chapter explores amusement, bittersweetness, nostalgia, cognitive dissonance, paradox, irony, and sarcasm.

Amusement is an interesting emotion. It is similar to happiness, but with a distinct element of playfulness and humor. This explains why it is so satisfying to tell someone that a distasteful joke is unpleasant by using the phrase, "I am not amused."

By using that word in particular, you are implying that the joke, which was supposed to be funny and lighthearted, was not only funny, but *not lighthearted.* This drives home the point that certain things should not be met with amusement.

Bittersweetness, as implied by its name, is a mix of happiness and sadness. There is usually an element of growth or change associated with feeling this emotion. For example, we are happy that our kids are growing and thriving, but we do not feel ready to send them to college. We are both happy and sad at the same time about the same thing.

Nostalgia is a word that was invented in order to describe patients (mostly soldiers) who were partly sick due to missing their homes or families. The word "nostalgia" was invented by Johannes Hofer, a medical student whose patients were ill with the particular emotion of homesickness.

While it is no longer used as a medical term, nostalgia has remained in our vocabulary as a way to reminisce and feel sad about good things in the past.

This emotion can be negative, however, when people use it to justify resisting social change. For example, feeling nostalgia for the "good ole days" is damaging when it refers to a time when those days weren't so good for everyone, like slavery, the Holocaust, human rights atrocities, or decades of DDT use. It is difficult and unhealthy to look with nostalgia on a time or circumstance that was harmful to someone or something else.

Cognitive dissonance happens when we feel such a paradox that we cannot even put it into words.

When we are feeling two paradoxical things at once, our minds are performing mental gymnastics to justify these conflicting emotions.

Cognitive dissonance often comes from a place of vulnerability. However, when we are able to overcome cognitive dissonance and marry the two sentiments, while removing the fear of vulnerability, we are much more likely to come up with a productive, creative solution.

Irony and sarcasm are very similar. In fact, they are two sides of the same coin. Using irony and sarcasm simply means assigning opposite meanings to the words being said. This can be done playfully (irony) or aggressively (sarcasm).

Sarcasm is a tool used by someone who is feeling frustrated or exasperated. They use sarcasm to make a point – essentially saying, "not only are you wrong, but you are also dumb for failing to see why." It is important that those who are speaking with young children, someone they just met, or someone during a heated argument avoid these hurtful, reactionary responses.

Irony and sarcasm usually boil down to a sentiment that requires honesty and reflection, not humor.

Key Points

1. Bittersweetness and nostalgia are both combinations of happiness and sadness, which manifest in different ways.

2. Cognitive dissonance happens when we are struggling to reconcile something we did or said, which we need to justify after the fact – this often leads to paradoxical thinking.

3. Irony and sarcasm are similar, but sarcasm has an extra bite of criticism.

Questions to Guide the Reader

1. How does amusement differ from happiness?

_____

_____

_____

_____

2. How are nostalgia and bittersweetness different?

_____
_____
_____
_____

3. What is a paradox?

_____
_____
_____
_____

4. How are sarcasm and irony different?

_____
_____
_____
_____

Action Plan

1. When experiencing nostalgia or bittersweetness, be sure to question yourself – are you yearning for something that was detrimental to someone or something else? Both of these emotions –nostalgia

and bittersweetness – can be experienced in positive and negative ways.

2. Remember to check yourself for cognitive dissonance. It may mean we're lying to ourselves about some sort of fact or decision from the past in order to justify our actions.

3. Beware of the use of sarcasm and irony with young children – they cannot understand the nuances of speech before some physical and mental maturity has occurred – usually around nine or ten years old.

Chapter Six: Places We Go When We're Hurting

Summary

This chapter explores anguish, hopelessness, despair, sadness, and grief.

Anguish is a very painful, powerful emotion. It is a combination of grief, powerlessness, and shock, and can even cause physical pain. For most of us, anguish sneaks up on us, and it seems unbearable. Anguish is painful, but it is an essential part of the human experience.

Hope is a function of thinking, rather than a true emotion. Hope is defined as a function of struggle – when we are struggling, hope takes over as a coping mechanism. While feeling hopeful is closely related to emotions, it is more primarily a cognitive pattern that occurs when we feel we have a helpful, realistic goal.

Hopelessness and despair are closely related, but again, not the same.

Hopelessness comes from our tendency to hyperfocus on disappointments. We feel hopeless when we feel ill-equipped to solve a specific problem.

Despair happens when we allow hopelessness to take over our lives.

The best way to combat hopelessness and despair is to focus on the three Ps: personalization, permanence, and pervasiveness.

Personalization happens because we feel as though our troubles are directed at us, either because of who we are, or because we feel alone in the struggle. We need to remember that most of our problems do not arise this way and the emotions we feel are not "personal".

Permanence is important because we often feel, in times of hopelessness and despair, that the problem will never be solved. This is almost never the case, despite how strongly we sometimes feel.

Pervasiveness simply means that whatever is ailing us is not all-encompassing of our nature. We are not permanently or fundamentally changed by what is ailing us.

Sadness, as uncomfortable and unpleasant of an experience as it is, defines one part of the human condition. Sadness is different from grief and depression, although both of those do include elements of sadness.

Without sadness, we would never feel happiness.

Grief is a complex emotion born of loss, longing, and feeling out of control. Grief is the loss of something or someone you loved. Grief is not an emotion that will necessarily go away, but it can be managed. It is always healthier to learn to live *with* grief rather than repressing it.

If grief is born of something that affects adaptation or takes away our control, it becomes complicated grief. Complicated grief sometimes requires professional treatment.

Key Points

1. Hope is a pattern of thinking. Hopelessness and despair are emotions.

2. Anguish is born of grief, sadness, and loss of control. It is powerful and can be all-encompassing for a brief time.

3. Grief is a powerful emotion born of loss, longing, and a feeling of being out of control; it can be severe enough to require professional treatment.

Questions to Guide the Reader

1. What is the difference between despair and hopelessness?

   _____
   _____
   _____
   _____

2. How can one inspire hope in themselves?

   _____
   _____
   _____
   _____

3. What is depression? What is grief? Are these synonyms of "sadness"? If not, how are they all different?

_____
_____
_____
_____

4. What is the difference between grief and complicated grief?

_____
_____
_____
_____

Action Plan

1. To escape hopelessness and despair, remember the three Ps: personalization, permanence, and pervasiveness. Whatever is causing hopelessness and/or despair, remember that it is not an issue with your character, it is not permanent, and it is not all-encompassing nor does it define your entire existence.

2. Grief is a complex emotion, which can be very detrimental to emotional health if it is not treated.

Grief needs to be acknowledged and worked through. If the emotional state of the aggrieved is severe enough, it may require professional treatment. If this is the case, finding a professional who specializes in **complicated grief** is best.

3. For those suffering from grief, hopelessness, or despair, these are complex emotions, and are all human experiences we must endure at some point in our lives. The most important thing to remember when dealing with these emotions is that they are not marks against our character. Keep in mind these emotions are all *different from depression*, which is commonly a state, not a temporary wave of emotion. However, just like those suffering from depression, anyone suffering from severe and complex grief, hopelessness, or despair should seek professional treatment.

Chapter Seven: Places We Go with Others

Summary

This chapter describes compassion, pity, empathy, sympathy, boundaries, and comparative suffering. While they are often used as synonyms, compassion and empathy are actually different experiences. Empathy, despite being commonly thought of as an emotion, is actually a skill that fuels *compassion* in us.

Compassion is a powerful, healing emotion, and should be practiced daily.

True empathy comes from compassion, and true compassion requires empathy. Compassion teaches us and increases our capacity for responsibility, improves our relationships, and actually makes decision-making easier. Opening ourselves up to compassion and building up our "reserves" of compassion to call upon when we need it is one of the most important methods of creating emotional stability.

Empathy is a skill we use to share in someone else's pain without trying to fix the problem. It is being fully present with someone who is suffering, taking on some of their pain, but not offering a solution or any actions.

What most people get tripped up on is trying to come up with solutions, when the person suffering simply needs someone to acknowledge and share their distress. This is especially true of parents. Of course, sometimes it is necessary for us to fix our children's problems, chase away the monsters, and just generally fight for them, but there are certainly other times when it is necessary to allow someone to feel the pain and consequences of their own actions. Learning when to apply different methods is a skill that benefits the empath, as well as the empathized party.

Showing others compassion and using empathy to help experience their pain creates connections between people. It also teaches the other person to do the same – practice compassion and develop their own empathy.

Empathy is a tool used to develop compassion between ourselves and others. It can be categorized as cognitive or affective.

Cognitive empathy is when someone has not experienced the pain that someone else has, but they use their compassion and imagination to put themselves in the other person's shoes. "I can imagine how that feels." Affective empathy occurs when someone *has* experienced the same type of pain, and can directly relate to it, "I know how that feels." Affective and cognitive empathy are important tools, as they both increase our capacity for compassion.

On the opposite side of empathy and compassion, we have sympathy and pity.

Pity is a harmful emotion. It creates a barrier between people. One person thinks "I feel bad for this person, but at least I will never have to experience what they are going through." When someone is pitied, they feel inferior, abandoned, helpless, and isolated. None of these feelings are helpful and they're certainly not healthy.

Sympathy is born of pity. It is often not genuine or beneficial, and it maintains the emotional barrier that keeps someone separated from another person's pain. Furthermore, feeling as though someone pities you or sympathizes without empathy or compassion can even trigger shame.

Along the finer points of empathy, there is a danger of enmeshment.

This happens when the empath does not have clear boundaries, and they fall so deep into someone else's pain they themselves cannot get out of it. The way to avoid this is by setting firm boundaries. While unclear/mutable boundaries may *seem* kind at the time, they will only lead to confusion and disappointment.

Comparative suffering is a cruel, hyperbolic manner of thinking. It is the act of someone thinking to themselves (or saying out loud), "She thinks she has it rough? I just got fired!" This sort of thinking heavily implies that the person complaining of their own pain does not acknowledge the pain other people feel as well, which is rarely the case. It is strictly an egocentric viewpoint.

Key Points

1. True compassion requires empathy, and true empathy only comes from compassion. This requires us to intentionally be present in someone else's pain, without judgment, asking questions (without interrupting), and genuinely experiencing and acknowledging the emotions expressed by the other party.

2. Pity is a harmful way of thinking and creates separation and barriers rather than connections between people. Sympathy is an emotion born of pity – it maintains the emotional separation, and is often more harmful than helpful.

3. Setting and maintaining boundaries are essential for healthy emotional relationships.

Questions to Guide the Reader

1. What is the difference between compassion and empathy? Should these words be used interchangeably or not?

_____
_____
_____
_____

2. Why is pity so harmful to people?

_____
_____
_____
_____

3. What is the difference between cognitive and affective empathy?

_____

_____

_____

_____

4. How does comparative suffering hurt or help the suffering party? (Tricky question!)

_____

_____

_____

_____

Action Plan

1. Practice compassion each day. The more it is practiced, the more naturally it will come, and the easier it will be to feel and share true empathy, which is a healing force in the world. Remember that cognitive and adaptive empathy are both useful tools.

2. Avoid pity. Pitying someone else creates a barrier, a sense of separation, and isolation of the pitied person. Avoiding pity also means not mistaking sympathy for empathy.

3. Sympathy is born of pity. Pity and sympathy will make the pitied person feel isolated and ashamed.

4. Maintaining emotional boundaries and practicing empathy and compassion rather than comparative suffering or pity are the most effective tools used in interpersonal relationships.

Chapter Eight: Places We Go When We Fall Short

Summary

This chapter discusses shame, self-compassion, perfectionism, guilt, humiliation, and embarrassment.

Shame is an extremely difficult emotion to talk about with others. It feels like we are inherently broken, bad, or missing something. However, the more we talk about it, the more we realize everyone has felt ashamed multiple times in their lives.

Shame isolates us; it makes us feel as though we are not as good as others.

However, once we start talking about it, we not only realize these feelings are inaccurate, but also that everyone feels this way sometimes. Shame is the opposite of empathy – it is the belief that we do not deserve love or are flawed in some way.

The cure for shame is practicing love and self-compassion.

Feeling shameful is an indicator that we need to show ourselves some love. This is because shame is an inward, self-involved emotion; therefore, we are the only ones capable of addressing it and realizing lasting change within ourselves.

Guilt is very similar to shame, but with a major difference. Instead of feeling as though *we are bad*, when we feel guilty, we feel as though *we did something bad.* Usually, the bad thing is that we lowered our own values or standards and disappointed someone – maybe yourself. Just like shame, guilt maintains the emotional barriers we are holding up, the same barriers empathy breaks down.

Humiliation and embarrassment: for most of us, we assume these two emotions are the same.

Unlike humiliation, embarrassment is generally a more lighthearted emotion. There is a spark of humor in it. We did something unflattering or we feel self-conscious for someone else, but no one is feeling terribly ashamed or pushed to the point of anger.

True embarrassment, not humiliation, is only experienced for a few moments at the most. The embarrassed party usually responds with humor, or an apology, or even just by breezing past the mistake.

Humiliation happens when we feel ridiculed by someone or a group. We feel self-righteous and wronged. There is an element of our dignity being harmed. We feel as though someone has pointed out a crucial flaw that does not exist, which leads to fury, frustration, and extreme embarrassment.

There is even research that shows humiliation leads to violence. In fact, every school shooter interviewed between 1996-1999 described feeling humiliated by their peers.

Perfectionism is often a point of pride in people. However, someone with perfectionist tendencies usually has acquired them through shame. Perfection is not achievable. It is bad for productivity and relationships when you have expectations for yourself and others that are far too high, so everything ends in disappointment.

We are all human. To expect perfection from our peers, loved ones, or ourselves will lead to disappointment.

Let go of perfectionism by changing your self-talk. Instead of focusing on "What will everyone think of me?", try thinking "How can I improve?" There is nothing wrong with wanting to improve - **the danger is in yearning for perfection.**

Key Points

1. Shame is a complex emotion that creates barriers between people. The ashamed party is almost always afraid to speak plainly about what they are feeling because they feel alone, as though they are the only person who has felt this way. They feel less secure and confident than those around them – embarrassed and undeserving. The irony is, once we start opening up and being honest about our shame, the more easily we can break down these barriers, and realize that everyone has felt ashamed at some point in their lives.

2. Perfectionism is a trait that many of us hold with pride, but it is actually born of shame.

3. Humiliation and embarrassment are often thought of as the same emotion, but they are different. Embarrassment is generally met with humor; the embarrassed party realizes the mistake is

something everyone has done. When someone is humiliated, on the other hand, they feel wronged and become furious.

Questions to Guide the Reader

1. What is the difference between guilt and shame? How are they similar?

_____
_____
_____
_____

2. What is self-compassion?

_____
_____
_____
_____

3. Define perfectionism and its roots.

_____
_____
_____
_____

Action Plan

1. In order to move through shame, you must begin with self-compassion and empathy. You need to be kind to yourself before you can heal from shame. Reach out and speak your truth.

2. Perfectionism is bad for productivity and social relationships – it will isolate someone and they will fail to meet even their own expectations. To combat perfectionism, rephrase from "What will people think of me?" to "How can I improve?" and reevaluate your expectations. You can still improve and set goals, but they need to be realistic so they are achievable!

3. Moving through guilt is similar to moving through shame. However, instead of reconnecting with yourself, you need to reconnect with another party. Practicing empathy and compassion toward the person you have disappointed (assuming the guilt is valid, and not perceived guilt) will heal the broken connection between the two parties.

Chapter Nine: Places We Go When We Search for Connection

Summary

This chapter will discuss belonging, fitting in, connection, disconnection, insecurity, invisibility, and loneliness.

Belonging is an important trait for the human animal. We are social creatures, and we require human connection in order to be happy and healthy. Consider Maslow's Hierarchy of Needs. In this order, human needs are defined as: physiological (food, water, shelter), safety, love/belonging, esteem, and self-actualization.

In order to experience true belonging, we must be able to show all of our true selves.

Connection and disconnection are both parts of the human experience. Connection is achieved from feeling a sense of true belonging. Disconnection can, and will, happen in every interpersonal relationship we have. This is not something that can be avoided.

What is important is how the disconnect is processed. It's important not to dismiss or ignore the disconnection. This will allow differences to grow and fester.

Ideally, these disconnects should be met with patience, so they may be addressed and used as a growing opportunity. In this way, disconnection serves us and allows us to deepen our relationships.

If not addressed, however, disconnection can become severe enough to cause physical pain and disempowerment. The reason this is so powerful is because the part of the brain that processes disconnection follows the same neural pathways as the sensation of feeling physical pain.

Others will perform mental gymnastics to avoid the pain of disconnection. They will tell themselves they are the exception and do not need relationships with other people – effectively pushing people away.

They will downplay their need for connection and, when an invitation is not extended due to inferred disinterest, they will blame the group or other party for not extending such an invitation.

Insecurity, at its root, is uncertainty about feeling loved, loving oneself, or having what we need for survival. Insecurity can be experienced as general insecurity, which is a state and a trait, domain insecurity (state), or relationship insecurity (state).

Domain insecurity comes from being uncertain of where our next meal will come from, or if we will be able to keep a roof over our heads. This sort of insecurity is detrimental to our health and survival.

Relationship insecurity can refer to a romantic relationship, a friendship, or any other interpersonal relationship. This is when we feel unsupported, perhaps lied to, or unsure of whether the people in our lives have a positive view of us.

The cure for insecurity as it relates to traits or relationships – *not* domain insecurity – is self-security. We need to learn to feel more sure of ourselves to avoid these problems.

Invisibility and loneliness and similar emotions, but invisibility takes the cake as one of the most painful experiences a human being can endure.

Invisibility comes from disconnection, with a dehumanizing element, leaving the afflicted person feeling pitied, unacknowledged, dismissed, or ignored, often in times of immediate need or crisis.

Loneliness is a feeling of being denied a social connection or attention when those connections and attention are readily available. We are wired to desire connection and belonging. Loneliness and invisibility are the cruel denials of these connections and support.

Living with loneliness is physically dangerous. We are social animals, and we need human connections to survive. Feeling chronic loneliness will dull our senses of hope and creativity, and can even impair executive functioning and skills.

Key Points

1. Belonging and connection are important social and evolutionary emotions required for humanity. As social creatures, we need to feel as though we are accepted, respected, and actively contributing to a group or setting we identify with.

2. Insecurity is inevitable, but working through it will lead to self-security.

3. Invisibility is one of the most painful experiences to endure.

Questions to Guide the Reader

1. What is Maslow's Hierarchy of Needs? Does the order of such needs surprise you in any way?

_____
_____
_____
_____

2. How can connection be therapeutic, and disconnection be harmful?

_____
_____
_____
_____

3. What is self-security?

_____
_____
_____
_____

4. How are loneliness and invisibility dangerous?

_____

_____

_____

_____

Action Plan

1. Remember to stay in touch with yourself when exploring the social and emotional needs of connection and belonging. Feeling a true sense of belonging and human connection is a healthy and important healing emotion. Do not fall into the trap of forcibly avoiding connections to protect your heart.

2. Refer to Maslow's Hierarchy of Needs when necessary, to remind yourself that connection and belonging are preceded ONLY by safety and physiological needs.

3. When battling insecurity, it's important (and painful, but necessary) to work through it. The process of overcoming insecurity is to accept our weaknesses and be kind to ourselves when reaching for self-security.

Chapter Ten: Places We Go When the Heart Is Open

Summary

This chapter discusses love, lovelessness, heartbreak, trust, self-trust, betrayal, defensiveness, flooding, and hurt.

While researchers are still debating whether love is a human experience or an emotion, there are a lot of important facts we do know about love.

Love is something we need and must nurture for our emotional health.

Love is the desire to connect with someone on an intimate level and make a commitment to that person. The complexities of love are endless and can be felt in many different ways and types of relationships.

Love can, and will, appear in our lives as intimate love, love for friends and family, even love for pets. Life without love is a dangerous way to live, as so many of our emotional needs stem from our need to experience – to give and to receive – love.

On the other hand, lovelessness is the need for "love ethics." This is a situation where we intuitively know that love is important, and could potentially solve a problem.

Heartbreak, although similar, is different from lovelessness. Heartbreak occurs when someone we have given our heart to dismisses us, rejects us, or fails to meet our expectations.

There is an enormous range of how powerful and hurtful heartbreak can be. It can be anything from a small wound all the way up to a debilitating, life-altering devastation.

At its core, heartbreak is the loss of love or the loss of what love could be. We feel heartbroken when a relationship ends, a pet passes on, and when a friend or loved one has let us down. Most of us fail to notice that there is an element of bravery in being heartbroken – in order to have had your heart broken, you must have opened your heart to love in the first place.

Trust is *incredibly* important in our relationships with others and with ourselves. The acronym BRAVING helps us identify all of the traits we must see in another before we can truly trust them.

- B is for boundaries. In order to trust someone or yourself, you must have and hold healthy boundaries. If boundaries are constantly being broken, this is a red flag that someone may not be trustworthy.

- R is for reliability. Can you trust someone if you do not find them reliable to do what they say they will do? No.

- A is for accountability. When mistakes happen, and they will, is the other person holding themselves accountable? If you are questioning your trust in yourself – are you holding yourself accountable?

- V is for vault. In order to trust someone, you need to know that sensitive information will be kept unshared or "in the vault."

- I stands for integrity. If you do not feel as though the person you are questioning has integrity, they are not likely to be trustworthy.

- N is for nonjudgmental. A trustworthy person is able to listen and remain nonjudgmental after information is shared that they may not necessarily agree with.

- G is for generosity. Is the person you wish to place your trust in a generous person – with their time, their heart, and their attention? If not, they may not be the right person to hold your trust. You must also learn to be generous to yourself, if you are struggling with feelings of not being able to trust yourself.

Betrayal is the emotion related to placing your trust in someone or something, then feeling let down. Betrayal is the loss or violation of trust. We can betray ourselves, betray others, and *be* betrayed by others. If history – and Shakespeare – have taught us anything, it is that, if the betrayal is large enough, it can actually cause trauma, up to and including death.

In order to heal, the betrayer must do the following: take responsibility and be accountable for the mistake that caused the breach in trust, make amends, and take action to prevent the same problem from occurring ever again.

Defensiveness is a tool we create inside ourselves to protect our ego or an attack on our character or self-worth. This is usually the result of having been betrayed in the past.

Flooding is what happens when we are totally overwhelmed emotionally and shut down. We can feel flooded by any emotion, but generally, the ensuing shutdown comes from being flooded with grief, despair, hopelessness, and many other detrimental emotions. While it is possible to have a flood of love or hope, these types of flooding generally do not cause an emotional shutdown.

Feeling hurt is an isolating and painful emotion.

When we are hurt, we feel vulnerable, aggrieved, and often have trouble talking to someone else about being hurt.

This is especially true if that person is the party who hurt us in the first place. Ironically, the best way to avoid being hurt in the same way *is* to talk to the offending party about being hurt, so they may avoid hurting you in the same way again in the future.

Key Points

1. Love is a blanket term for the strong, unshakable connection we feel for another person, while lovelessness reflects a lack of love for ourselves as well as between us and others.

2. Building trust is important and can be broken down into several assets, which will help identify where the bond is lacking in order to strengthen it. Use the acronym BRAVING (boundaries, reliability, accountability, vault, integrity, nonjudgmental, generosity).

3. Betrayal is the loss of trust in someone or something. Betrayal is powerful and detrimental to our health. It can cause emotional and even physical harm or trauma.

4. Hurt feelings and flooding are mechanisms of our interpersonal relationships. We cannot experience hurt feelings without another person being involved, and it is usually someone close to us. Flooding is a state of complete overwhelm, brought on by a conflict that involves someone else.

Questions to Guide the Reader

1. Explain a circumstance in which someone may experience lovelessness and how that can affect a person.

_____

_____

_____

_____

2. How is heartbreak different from lovelessness?

_____

_____

_____

_____

3. What does BRAVING stand for, and what does each
   term mean in relation to building trust?

_____

_____

_____

_____

4. How are defensiveness and self-esteem related?
   How can self-esteem help prevent defensiveness?

_____

_____

_____

_____

Action Plan

1. While love is widely recognized as good and a powerful healing tool, most of us forget to practice it. Fill your days, your life, and your relationships with love and watch them become stronger and deeper.

2. If a relationship needs strengthening, use the acronym BRAVING to identify any weaknesses in your ability to trust someone or for someone else to trust you.

3. If someone has betrayed your trust, the only way to heal is for that person to acknowledge the pain they've caused, make amends, and take action to fix the problem and avoid future betrayal.

4. The solution to defensiveness, which functions as protection for our self-esteem, is **grounded confidence** – a difficult and powerful tool, in which you accept your weaknesses, and believe that they are simply human nature and not a fundamental flaw in your character.

Chapter Eleven: Places We Go When Life Is Good

Summary

The emotions studied in this chapter are joy, happiness, calm, contentment, gratitude, foreboding joy, relief, and tranquility.

Joy and happiness are different emotions. Joy is a short burst of pleasurable contentment, love, happiness, and appreciation. It is often felt in conjunction with another person, connecting with nature, experiencing a religious revelation, or feeling at peace with one's surroundings.

Unlike joy, happiness is a steady emotion and is a trait, not a state.

This means that external sources cannot and will not provide true happiness. Happiness needs to be nurtured and come from within.

Feeling calm is actually an effect of mindfulness, which includes maintaining a clear perspective on a situation despite any chaos happening around it.

Contentment is similar to feeling calm, but has a few hallmarks of its own. We feel content when we feel as though we are enough. It is also a low-arousal emotion, which simply means it often occurs in the background. Contentment is an underrated goal for many of us, but it is very valuable and helps us nurture our confidence, happiness, and satisfaction.

Gratitude is another underrated emotion, but one that is powerful and has healing properties. Fostering and practicing gratitude on a daily basis will change the way you think and live. You will feel more connected to yourself and others as well.

Foreboding joy is a complex phenomenon that occurs when we feel afraid to lean into a joyful moment or feel free, happy, or relaxed. There is an element of feeling guarded, sure that the situation is "too good to be true."

While not often spoken about, this is an emotion that almost everyone feels at some point in their lives. It functions to protect ourselves from disappointment. However, it is harmful.

By letting this become a habit, we will actually impair our ability to feel the things we are afraid of accepting – love, happiness, relaxation, and contentment.

The best way to combat this is to practice gratitude daily. This will reinforce deep within you that the good things in life are yours, they are earned, they are deserved, and you are allowed to enjoy them.

Relief is the feeling we have when we let go of tension and experience the safety and freedom to breathe after a stressful experience or situation.

Tranquility is a beautiful and often overlooked emotion. When we are tranquil, we are actually feeling the absence of pressure or demand (for our time, attention, or work). This is similar to contentment, with one key difference. Contentment tends to describe relaxation we feel we have earned, while tranquility describes feeling relaxation that comes from having no pressure to do anything.

Key Points

1. Joy is a specific, brief, and intense wave of pleasure – different from happiness, which is a trait that can be nurtured. External sources are not responsible for happiness, while joy is often sparked by external sources, such as nature, the universe, or a deep connection to someone else.

2. Calmness, like happiness, needs to be nurtured. It is maintained by mindfulness. Contentment, although similar, is a low-arousal emotion that helps us measure the satisfaction of our lives. Contentment is often correlated with calmness, as well as happiness and confidence.

3. Gratitude is a powerful tool used to heal foreboding joy and dissatisfaction with our lives. In addition, it can foster a greater tolerance for embracing vulnerability.

Questions to Guide the Reader

1. What is the difference between happiness and joy? Do either or both come from internal or external sources?

_____

_____

_____

_____

2. How is gratitude a healing emotion? Why is it so
   powerful?

_____

_____

_____

_____

3. What is foreboding joy? Why is it harmful?

_____

_____

_____

_____

4. What is the difference between contentment and
   tranquility?

_____

_____

_____

_____

Action Plan

1. Wishing or wanting joy and happiness for someone else is very powerful. This is likely one of the kindest gifts we can give each other. As discussed in previous chapters, try to fill your life with love and connection, and this includes rooting for the people we love to feel these powerfully positive, healing emotions.

2. Calmness, like happiness, needs to come from within. We need to nurture our ability to feel calm, often with meditation and mindfulness practices. Next to fostering calmness, practicing gratitude is another important and powerful emotion. Gratitude journals, for example, are a great way to incorporate this powerful tool.

3. Foreboding joy is an uncomfortable, but universal, emotion characterized by being apprehensive or afraid to accept a joyful moment. Most of us have felt this at one time or another, although we might assume we are the only ones who feel this way. The best way to overcome this powerful, negative emotion is to practice gratitude. This will increase our capacity to feel good things and strengthen our tolerance for feeling vulnerable.

Chapter Twelve: Places We Go When We Feel Wronged

Summary

This chapter explores anger, contempt, disgust, dehumanization, hate, and self-righteousness.

Anger is a complex emotion. It can range from mild to severe in degree and has the tendency to "take over" even the mildest mannered of us all because it is a high-arousal emotion.

Anger takes place in the nervous system, which is why we often feel as though we are flooded with anger, and can feel its physical effects on the body.

This is why when we are angry, we feel as though we must *do* something to alleviate our rage. It can also lead to many other negative emotions, several of which we'll discuss in this chapter. Anger is often a masking emotion for other problems like confusion, betrayal, isolation, sadness, injustice, jealousy, depression, and many more.

It's not all bad, though. Anger can be a powerful catalyst for change – specifically social change. Every major revolution in world history has its roots in anger and a determined unwillingness to allow things to remain the same. However, anger is especially painful to hold onto over time. It should be released after our point is made, we feel heard, and change has begun.

Contempt is a form of hate that occurs when someone feels fundamentally superior to another. This is a very powerful and harmful emotion - it leads to deep psychological wounds, a breakdown of trust, and a forced distance or barrier between people.

Within a marriage, a common example of contempt is when one person communicates to the other that they hate something they did, who they are, or what they represent, with the specific intent to harm the other person's concept of themself.

When we think of disgust, we generally think of a function in our brains that protects us from ingesting something poisonous, e.g., moldy food or off-smelling water will spark disgust and revulsion. However, as disgust moves closer to contempt, an element of dehumanization is introduced.

Disgust + contempt = an unreasonable and unfair hatred of someone or a group. This is a slippery slope and one where the damage often cannot be reversed.

Dehumanization is one of the most dangerous emotions that humans are capable of. It changes our wiring - set in place to make sure we do not harm, degrade, or kill our own kind.

This type of change is dangerous and permanent, and is also a slippery slope, similar to contempt – once we break down those internal rules, the less inhibited a person feels about harming another.

Hate itself is a triggering word for some because it is such a dangerous place for their heart to be. Hate is sneaky - in order for it to survive, it must fester and spread from person to person. Hate is how an entire country can become contemptuous of another.

Hate is actually fueled by our need for human connection. Despite its dangerous qualities, it is still a function of society that brings people together, for better or for worse.

Self-righteousness is a complicated emotion that is often mislabeled. It happens when we try to convince ourselves or others that we are doing the right thing, even if it is clear we aren't. This is simply a way for us to justify our own behavior. (Note: self-righteousness is *not* the same thing as righteousness. Righteousness is the urge to fix a societal problem or take action for a genuinely good reason.)

Key Points

1. Anger and contempt are different. Anger is a catalyst, born of a lot of other negative emotions, including shame, fear, humiliation, and more. Anger is often a catalyst for change. Contempt is anger with an intentional message to another person as being inferior – incapable of change or unworthy of its effort.

2. Dehumanization and hate are destructive emotions that need to be checked and avoided.

3. Hate is a catalyst emotion, like anger. It likes to spread. However, if people do not actively circulate it, it dies.

Questions to Guide the Reader

1. Why is contempt, specifically, so harmful in a marriage – as compared to frustration, anger, or disappointment?

   _____
   _____
   _____
   _____

2. How can disgust lead to dehumanization?

   _____
   _____
   _____
   _____

3. In what way does hate spread within a community?

   _____
   _____
   _____
   _____

Action Plan

1. Avoid contempt, avoid any person who treats you with contempt, and if you feel you are contemptuous of others or are beginning to think or communicate in contemptuous ways, it's time to see a professional! Contempt is a dangerous and harmful emotion. Contempt cannot lead to resolution. The only way to move on with any conflict is to let go of contempt and cruelty.

2. Disgust is an important tool for protecting against something poisonous, toxic, or otherwise harmful to our well-being. While it may feel like a negative emotion – and, in many ways, it is -- disgust is used to warn us of danger, both physical and social. Disgust can steer us clear of offensive behaviors like racism. However, it can also turn someone the other way, and steer them toward feelings of dehumanization, a harmful and violent emotion. The only way to combat this is to be aware of and correct dangerous language in others and within ourselves – language matters and is always the catalyst for dehumanization and hate.

3. Self-righteousness is a red flag – it's often used as a way to make an exception for ourselves, or to ourselves. This boils down to lying to ourselves and to others, which is harmful to our own emotional health and our relationships. This behavior can be combated by nurturing your self-confidence.

Chapter Thirteen: Places We Go to Self-Assess

Summary

The final chapter of the book describes pride, hubris, and humility.

Pride is an emotion that a lot of people think of as negative. However, pride is actually simply the pleasure and celebration we feel after an accomplishment or achievement. There is nothing wrong with true pride, as long as it celebrates something positive we have done.

Hubris is what most people are actually speaking of when they think of pride as negative. Hubris is an inflated sense of unearned pride. It comes from shame – the fear of not being capable or worthy, which often comes across as aggressive or competitive.

Humility, by contrast, is openness. Humility allows us to open up about not having the information necessary to solve a problem or understand something. Again, this emotion is often wrongfully labeled as negative. The negativity comes when someone is unwilling to be honest about their own gaps in information.

Key Points

1. Humility and pride are often thought of as negative emotions, but are perfectly healthy in reality.

2. Hubris is born of shame.

3. Humility describes the honesty someone has in communicating that they need assistance.

Questions to Guide the Reader

1. If you are experiencing a wave of pleasure after getting an A on a tough exam, are you feeling hubris or pride?

_____
_____
_____
_____

2. How are pride and hubris often regarded, and why is the general perception untrue?

_____
_____
_____
_____

3. What is humility? Is it related to humiliation?

_____
_____
_____
_____

Action Plan

1. Self-assessment can be difficult, but it is necessary. Always be sure to check in with yourself when reflecting.

2. Pride and hubris often look the same to other people – be sure to check in with yourself if you're accused of hubris. You may be confusing the two and need to adjust your perspective.

3. Practice humility as often as possible. Admitting that you don't understand something is the most effective way to learn.

Conclusion

Atlas of the Heart is a book of its own genre. This book is perfect for mental health caregivers, leaders, parents, anyone undergoing a major life change, and pretty much anyone else who is interested in how their own emotions work.

Have you ever wanted to be able to break down and track what got you to a certain unpleasant state, such as rage, jealousy, contempt, or aggression? Have you ever wondered why feeling loved is so powerful? How about whether or not someone is trustworthy? These questions and anything else related to how we *feel* can be answered within this text.

Brown writes in a clear, concise manner. This book is enjoyable and can be easily digested by nearly anyone. The way the book is structured, around groups of related emotions, is the first lesson of this book.

Just looking at the chapter titles can give some answers on which type of emotions someone may want to explore. Identifying whether or not an emotion belongs to a certain group - some of the combinations and definitions of different emotions in this book may be a surprise!

Diving deep into our emotional health is not only difficult, but terrifyingly ignored by many people. The reasons behind this can come from ignorance, fear, and issues with facing our own demons, among others.

Our emotions, how we experience them, and any hitches or gaps, are a huge part of the guiding forces of our lives.

Most of us are aware of this on some level, but few of us are brave enough to actually do the work to understand them, much less become their master and harness their impact.

This book can be useful for so many people. If any of the following applies to you, you may benefit from reading this book or recommending it to someone you know who:

- Has problems with addiction

- Has problems with self-control

- Has difficulties in intimate relationships

- Struggles with trust

- Struggles with outbursts of negative emotion

- Has problems maintaining interpersonal relationships

- Has problems maintaining romantic, intimate relationships

- Is curious about how one emotion can lead to the next

- Has problems with communication in your work life

- Wants to understand human connections on a deeper level

- Wants to advance in their career, but are convinced they do not have the confidence to do so

- Struggles with self-contempt

- Wishes to open up more to your friends and loved ones

If any of those sound familiar, then this message is for you. This book is a perfect example of one that can be read multiple times and the reader will discover new meanings each time.

Background Information About Atlas of the Heart

As one of Brown's many bestsellers, the inspiration for this particular book came from her desire to define and explore the 87 different emotions and human experiences she catalogued. This book was written in order to create accurate language about emotions, and clarify some of the problems with different verbiage for similar emotions.

Brown set out to explain the differences and define every emotion that humans can experience. This was a goal for her, in order to share her knowledge and create a book like no other. This material can be referenced when properly explaining what someone is feeling or experiencing, with no guesswork or incorrect language involved.

Background Information About Brené Brown

Brown was born on November 18, 1965, in San Antonio, Texas, to Charles Arthur Brown and Casandra Deanne Rogers. She is the oldest of four siblings. Although she was raised Catholic, Brown has since converted to Episcopalian. Brown married Steve Austin in 1987, has two children and lives in Houston, Texas. She opted to keep her maiden name when marrying.

Brown has a Bachelor's Degree in Social Work, a Master's Degree in Social Work, and a Doctorate of Philosophy in Social Work. All of her degrees come from the University of Texas at Austin or the University of Houston.

She is the author of six bestsellers, including this one, her newest, *Atlas of the Heart.* Brown performed a Ted Talk in 2010, titled "The Power of Vulnerability." She is also CEO of The Daring Way, a professional, certified training program.

Brown has had her own troubles with addiction and enrolled in AA after achieving her Master's Degree. She often speaks of how sobriety has changed her life for the better.

Awards and Accolades Held by the Author

Brown has achieved a lot in her career. In order, her awards and accolades include the following:

- In 2009, Houston Women's Magazine named her one of the city's Most Influential Women.

- In 2014, Brown won an Outstanding Faculty Award for her teaching at the Graduate College of Social Work.

- In 2016, the National Association of Social Workers awarded her the International Rhoda G. Sarnat Award.

- In 2017, she was named Time magazine's Person of the Year.

- In 2018, she was recognized again in Time magazine as one of the world's 100 Most Influential People.

- In 2019, she was awarded the Sydney Peace Prize.

- Also in 2019, Brown was awarded Harvard University's Gleitsman Award.

- Finally, again in 2019, Brown was awarded the Ridenhour Courage Prize.

Discussion Questions

1. How can this book be used to improve your understanding of yourself? Try to come up with at least three different methods.

2. If you were in a situation where someone breaks your trust, how can you rebuild it?

3. Is defensiveness a positive or a negative trait?

4. Is anxiety a trait, a state, or both?

5. Why is human connection so important, and how can this book help you improve your relationships?

6. The author describes contempt as one of the most dangerous emotions someone can feel. Why is that?

7. The author describes invisibility as one of the most painful emotions someone can feel. Why is that?

8. What are some examples of emotions that are often thought of as interchangeable, but actually are not?

9. What is the difference between a trait and a state?

10. What is the difference between an emotion and a human experience?

11. What is the difference between an emotion and cognitive functions, such as hope?

12. Does someone need to be diagnosed with an anxiety disorder in order to experience anxiety? Why or why not?

13. How can we cope with disappointment, failure, discouragement, and frustration? How are all of these emotions similar, and different?

14. Is curiosity the same thing as interest? Why or not why?

15. How long does someone typically feel surprised?

16. How is sympathy a potentially harmful emotion?

17. How can we cope with grief, and when does grief need to be treated by a professional?

18. Why should we avoid using sarcasm when speaking with young children? What does sarcasm achieve and why can it be confusing to some people?

19. Describe Maslow's Hierarchy of Needs.

20. What does the acronym "BRAVING" stand for, and for what problem is it used?

More books from Smart Reads

Summary of Breath: The New Science of a Lost Art By James Nestor

Workbook for What Happened to You? By Oprah Winfrey and Dr. Bruce Perry

Workbook for Atomic Habits By James Clear

Workbook for Limitless By Jim Kwik

Workbook for The Body Keeps the Score By Dr. Bessel van der Kolk

Workbook for Can't Gurt Mer By David Goggins

Thank You

Hope you've enjoyed your reading experience.

We here at Smart Reads will always strive to deliver to you the highest quality guides.

So I'd like to thank you for supporting us and reading until the very end.

Before you go, would you mind leaving us a review on Amazon?

It will mean a lot to us and support us creating high quality guides for you in the future.

Thanks once again!

Warmly yours,

The Smart Reads Team

Download Your Free Gift

As a way to say "Thank You" for being a fan of our series, I've included a free gift for you:

Brain Health: How to Nurture and Nourish Your Brain For Top Performance

Go to www.smart-reads.com to get your FREE book.

The Smart Reads Team

Made in the USA
Las Vegas, NV
01 October 2022

56356392R10049